HANDMADE by ME

Duct Tape DIY

Alix Wood

PowerKiDS
press.

Published in 2020 by Rosen Publishing
29 East 21st Street, New York, NY 10010

Copyright © 2020 Alix Wood Books

Editor: Eloise Macgregor
Designer: Alix Wood

Projects devised and created by Rebecca Wood and Ben Wood

Photo Credits: Cover, 1, 3, 5 top, 6, 7, 14, 15, 16, 17 © Alix Wood; 4, 5 bottom
© Adobe Stock Images; 8, 9, 10, 11, 22, 23, 24, 25, 32 © Rebecca Wood; 12, 13,
18, 19, 20, 21, 26, 27, 28, 29 © Ben Wood

Cataloging-in-Publication Data

Names: Wood, Alix.
Title: Duct tape DIY / Alix Wood.
Description: New York : PowerKids Press, 2020. | Series: Handmade by me |
Includes glossary and index.
Identifiers: ISBN 9781725302983 (pbk.) | ISBN 9781725303003 (library bound)
| ISBN 9781725302990 (6pack)
Subjects: LCSH: Tape craft--Juvenile literature. | Duct tape--Juvenile
literature.
Classification: LCC TT869.7 W65 2020 | DDC 745.5--dc23

Manufactured in the United States of America

CPSIA Compliance Information: Batch #: CSPK19
For Further Information contact Rosen Publishing, New York, New York at 1-800-237-9932

Contents

Meet the Amazing Duct Tape!

It is incredible how many really stylish gifts you can make using duct tape. Duct tape is tough, **water-resistant**, and you can buy it in many different colors and patterns.

Some projects in this book are done using **washi tape**. Found in craft stores, it is cheap and comes in tons of patterns and colors. Use duct tape instead if you don't have washi tape.

You Will Need ...

- duct tape
- washi tape
- scissors
- PVA glue
- card stock
- a hole punch
- other everyday household items, such as string, markers, chip containers, and some ribbon

How To Cut Duct Tape

Some people rip duct tape to the size they want. In this book we suggest using scissors. It creates a cleaner edge and helps keep the tape from getting in a tangle. To cut your tape, unroll it to the length you need. Lightly place it, sticky side down, on a flat surface. A **cutting mat** or clean chopping board is ideal. Then measure and cut your length. Keep both ends **taut** as you lift it, so it doesn't tangle.

Sticky Scissors?

Scissors can get gummed up cutting duct tape. You can clean the blades in a number of ways. **Spray lubricant**, rubbing alcohol, white vinegar, and even peanut butter all help remove sticky residue. Put your chosen substance on a thick cloth and gently wipe the blades. Don't press on the sharp edge of the blade, or you might cut yourself.

Duct Tape Basics

One of the best ways to use duct tape is to make it into a sheet of fabric. You can use duct tape fabric to make just about anything that you could make from cloth.

These steps show you how to make the fabric you will need for many of the projects in this book.

You Will Need ...

- duct tape
- masking tape
- a cutting mat or chopping board
- a ruler
- scissors

1

◀ Measure a strip of tape at least 1 inch (2.5 cm) longer than the width of fabric you need. Lightly place the tape sticky side down onto a cutting mat or old chopping board.

2

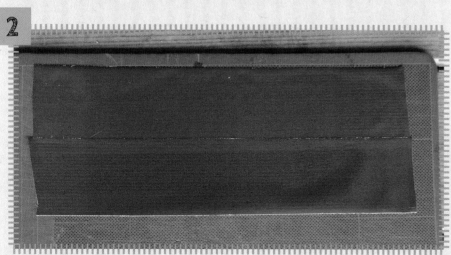

◀ Cut your first strip. Then cut and lay a second strip that slightly overlaps the first along the long edge. Continue adding strips until you have the size of fabric you need.

3

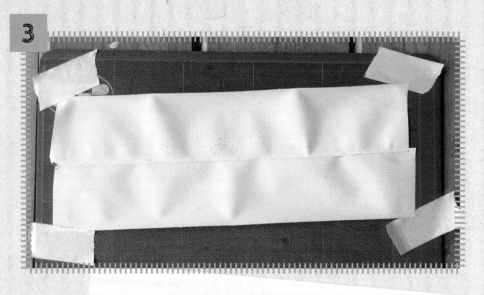

Have four strips of masking tape ready. Carefully turn your fabric over. Get one hand free from the sticky tape and put masking tape at each corner. Keep the ends apart so they don't stick together.

In a Sticky Mess?

One of the hardest things about working with duct tape is trying to get it off you! The masking tape trick above helps get your fingers free from the sticky side.

4

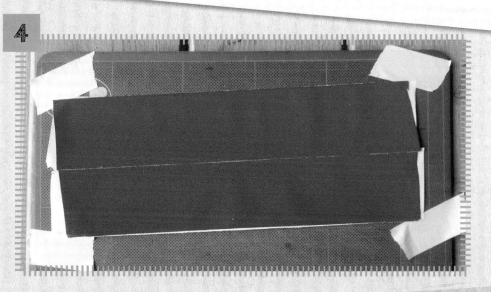

Follow steps 1 and 2 and make a second sheet. Place this sheet carefully, sticky side down, on top of the first sheet. Now trim your fabric to the size you need.

MORE IDEAS

You can make colorful **reversible** fabric, too. Just use a different color tape at step 4.

Kitchen Holder

This container can be used all over the house to keep things tidy. It is great in the kitchen for holding spaghetti, or for storing kitchen utensils. If you know an artist, they could keep their paintbrushes in it, too!

1

▲ Wrap some patterned tape around the top edge of your chip container. Overlap the ends slightly and cut the tape.

2

◄ Starting at the join of your first row of tape, wrap a wide piece of tape neatly underneath, touching or slightly overlapping the first row.

3

Continue covering the tube in the same way by adding a second thin strip of tape.

4

▲ Turn the tube around and start covering the other end.

Fill the center gap using a mix of the thin strips.

MORE IDEAS

Cover the container lid top using strips of wide tape. Cut away the **excess** using scissors. Then cover the lip with thin tape.

Phone Case

Just about everyone would love this duct tape case as a gift. A duct tape case is water-resistant, and helps protect against scratches and little accidents. It's easy to make, too.

1

▲ Make two pieces of duct tape fabric, 1 inch (2.5 cm) wider and the same height as the phone you wish to cover.

You Will Need ...

- wide duct tape
- thin patterned duct tape
- scissors
- ruler

2

▲ Join your two pieces of fabric lengthwise, using a strip of the same color tape.

3

▲ Fold one side over the other and seal the side and bottom of your case using more tape.

4

Add some trim to the open end using a length of the thin patterned duct tape. Overlap the tape over the open edge as shown.

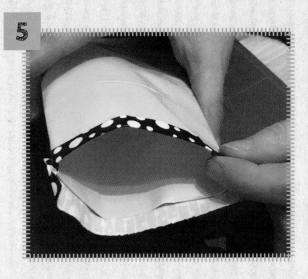

5

Once you have added trim all around the top, fold the overlap onto the inside of the case to cover the edge.

MORE IDEAS

You can use this same method to make all kinds of cases. Why not make a sunglasses case or a tablet case for someone as a gift? Just measure the sunglasses or tablet and make the case a tiny bit larger.

11

Bookmarks

Do you know a **bookworm**? Bookmarks are very easy to make and make excellent gifts. Try these two different styles, sure to please any reader.

1

▲ Draw two 2.5-inch (6.4 cm) squares on a piece of card stock. Divide one of the squares into two triangles. Cut out one square and one triangle.

2

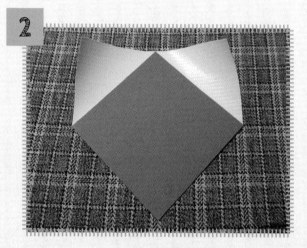

▲ Cover one side of the square with duct tape. Fold any excess over the back. Don't worry if the back looks messy. You will cover it later.

The finished corner bookmark

3

▲ Cut a strip of **contrasting** color tape and stick it to the triangle. Fold the bottom edge over.

4

▲ With the triangle over one corner of your square, fold the strip's flaps around the back to secure the triangle in place.

5

◀ Cover the messy back of the square with tape.

Cut around a penny to make circle decorations for your bookmark. ▶

6

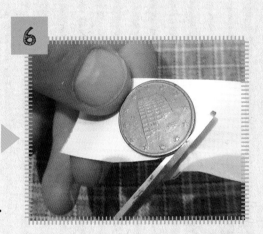

MORE IDEAS

Try making this **embossed** bookmark. Cut some shapes from card stock. Lay them onto the sticky side of a strip of tape. You could make a border using string. Lay a second strip of tape sticky side down over your design. Rub the tape with your finger to bring out the raised design.

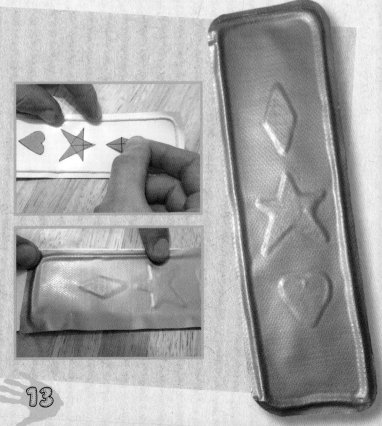

Tile Ornament

This decorated tile makes a great plant stand or ornament. Put someone's initial on it to make it a really personal gift.

1

▲ Cut four strips of tape, just shorter than the tile's width.

You Will Need ...

- plain tile
- washi tape
- scissors
- PVA glue
- pencil, paper, and marker
- old paintbrush

2

▲ Carefully stick the tape onto the tile to form an inner square. Trim any untidy corners.

3

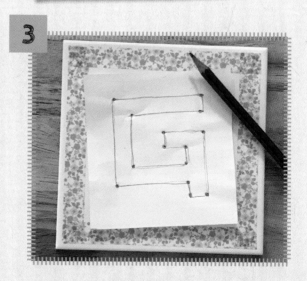

▲ Draw your chosen initial onto paper using rectangle shapes. Make a hole with a pencil in every corner.

4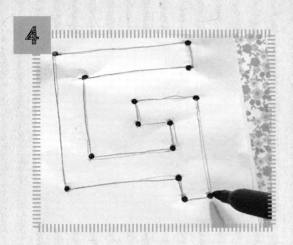

▲ Lightly tape your initial onto your tile. Using a marker, make a dot through each hole.

5

▲ Using your drawing and dots as a guide, make up your letter using lengths of tape. Then lift the corners and wipe away the dots.

6

▲ With an old paintbrush, **seal** the tile by painting all over it using PVA glue.

MORE IDEAS

Firmly tape a piece of string to the back of your tile, as shown. Now you can hang your tile on the wall.

Party Bunting

Bunting really adds to the fun atmosphere at a party or celebration. Why not surprise someone on their birthday with a homemade decoration?

You Will Need ...

- wide duct tape
- ribbon or string
- masking tape
- pencil and paper
- hole punch

1

▲ Using wide duct tape, make some pieces of fabric, two strips deep.

2 Trace this shape onto some paper. Then cut out the shape to use as your heart template.

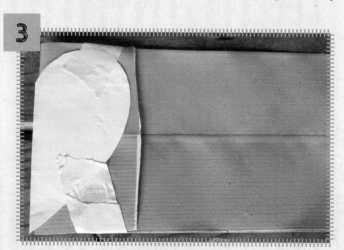

3

▲ Fold the end of a fabric strip over. Tape your cutout along the fold, as shown.

4

▲ Carefully cut around the shape using scissors.

▲ Opened out, the cutouts will be heart-shaped.

▲ Make a hole at the top of each side of the heart shapes using a hole punch.

Thread ribbon or string through the holes and hang your bunting.

MORE IDEAS

To make tiny bunting, fold rectangles of washi tape over a thin length of string. Cut the rectangles into triangles. Cut away from the string so you don't accidentally cut it, too!

Duct Tape Wallet

This cool wallet makes a useful present. It is not difficult to make. It looks so good your friends and family won't believe you made it from duct tape!

You Will Need ...

- wide duct tape
- thin duct tape
- scissors
- ruler
- cardboard and a piece of string (optional)

1

▲ Make a rectangle of duct tape fabric that you can trim to 9 inches (23 cm) by 6 inches (15 cm).

2

▲ Cut two lengths of tape slightly longer than the long sides of your rectangle.

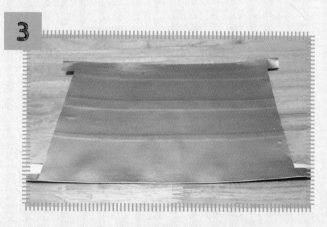

3

▲ Fold a strip over each long edge to cover it. Cut off any excess. Then fold your rectangle in half lengthwise.

4

▲ Make the pockets from two pieces of 4 x 2-inch (10 x 5 cm) tape fabric. Cover the top edges with another color tape.

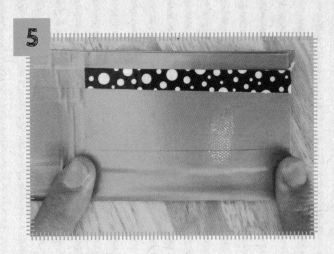

5

▲ Cut off any excess trim. Line up the first pocket near the top of the wallet. Tape it along the bottom.

6

◀ Tape the second pocket below the first, in line with the bottom of the wallet. Then tape the left-hand side.

MORE IDEAS

You could add a patch with an embossed initial. See page 13 for how to do this.

7

Finally, tape over either side of the long main pocket using your contrasting tape.

▼

Checkerboard

Do you know a chess or checkers fan? This handmade checkerboard would make a great gift.

You Will Need ...

- two or three different 2-inch-wide (5 cm) duct tapes
- a ruler and a pen
- some scissors
- a penny (optional)

1

▲ Make a 10-inch (25 cm) sheet of duct tape fabric. Using a ruler, mark out a 9-inch (23 cm) square and cut it out using scissors.

2

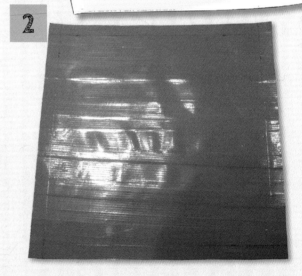

▲ Draw an inner square, half an inch from the edge all around. This will be your playing surface.

3

◄ Cut an 18-inch (46 cm) strip of the other tape. Draw a line lengthwise dividing the strip in half. Then draw a line across every inch (2.5 cm) to make 32 1-inch (2.5 cm) squares.

▲ Cut out your squares. Stick them to the marked playing surface, leaving 1 inch (2.5 cm) between each, as shown.

▲ Stagger your squares in each row, as shown, to make a checkerboard pattern.

MORE IDEAS

You could make your play pieces out of duct tape cloth. Draw around a penny and cut 12 circles of each color.

▲ You can frame your board with a contrasting tape and then cut off the excess.

You can use chocolate or candy as your play pieces. When you jump over a piece, you can eat it!

Drink Coasters

Coasters are a really cool gift for anyone's bedroom or home. You can make some using duct tape and washi tape in colors and styles you think the person will love.

You Will Need ...

- duct tape and washi tape
- scissors
- cardboard, or an old coaster or bathroom tile
- PVA glue
- old paintbrush

1

▲ If using cardboard, trace around a coaster or draw a 4-inch (10 cm) square onto some thick cardboard. Cut out your shape using scissors.

2

▲ Cover your cardboard, old coaster, or tile with strips of duct tape. Overlap the edges and then neatly trim around them using scissors.

3

◄ Choose tapes that look good with your main color. Stick the strips **diagonally** across the coaster. Fold the ends over underneath. Don't worry if the back looks messy. You will cover it up later.

4

Cover the back with strips of duct tape. Cut the strips neatly to fit.

5

To seal your coaster, paint the top with PVA glue. Washi tape doesn't stick well to shiny duct tape, so you may want to dab glue under some of those strips, too.

MORE IDEAS

Why not make your coaster match the color of your friend or family member's favorite mug?

Tube Drum

Do you know a young musician who would love their own drum? Make one using an old cardboard snack tube or piece of plastic drainpipe. Decorate it with colorful tape.

1

▲ Ask an adult to take the metal bottom off the snack tube using a can opener. Skip this stage if you are using drainpipe or a cardboard tube without a bottom.

You Will Need ...

- cardboard tube or piece of drainpipe (If you use a snack tube you'll need a can opener and an adult to help you)
- duct tape and scissors
- and old paintbrush and a pebble

2

◀ Choose your duct tape. Overlap the first strip and fold it over inside the tube to cover the edge. As you add more strips, line up the ends so they will all be on one side of the drum.

3

Keep adding your duct tape until you reach the top. You can overlap the top layer, too, but you don't have to. You will cover this later.

4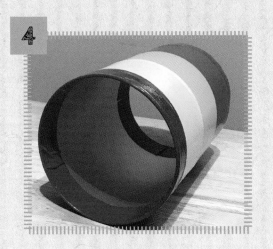

You should now have a tape-covered hollow tube.

5

To make the drumskin, lay overlapping strips of tape over the top of the tube. Overlap the side by around half an inch (1 cm). Trim off any excess, and cover the messy ends with another strip of tape.

MORE IDEAS

You could make a double-ended drumstick using a paintbrush and a pebble. Wrap the pebble in a square of duct tape. Secure it to the paintbrush handle with more tape. Each end will produce a different drum sound.

Small Tote Bag

This useful tote bag can be an overnight bag or a gift bag. As it is water-resistant, it would make a great beach bag, too. You could even display a houseplant in it.

You Will Need ...

- duct tape
- scissors
- a ruler
- double-sided tape

1 Make two same-size fabric squares. Then make a strip that is three times as long as one of your square's sides. Tape the middle of the strip to the two squares as shown.

We made our strips' and squares' reverse sides pink or yellow, to make the bag look more colorful.

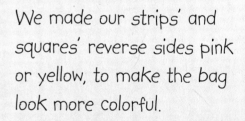

2

To make the bag shape, tape the left-hand part of the strip to the two squares' left-hand sides. Tape the right-hand part of the strip to the right-hand sides.

3

▲ Once you have taped your sides, your bag should look like the one above. Then turn your bag inside out, so the taped parts are on the inside.

4

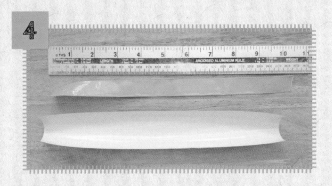

▲ To make the handles, cut two long strips of tape. Fold them in half lengthwise.

5

▲ Tape the handles to the inside of your bag.

MORE IDEAS

Add some decoration to your bag. You could make duct tape spots or stripes, or add some lace. We stuck lace onto our bag using double-sided tape.

A Bunch of Roses

These duct tape roses look like beautiful **porcelain**. They are simple to create and make great gifts.

You Will Need ...

- red, pink, and green duct tape
- thin wire
- scissors
- an adult to help you
- markers

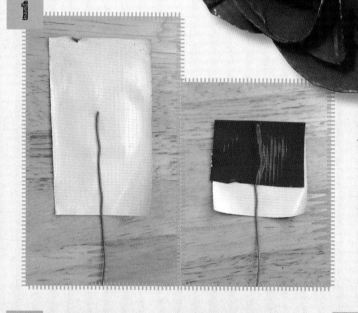

1

▶ Ask an adult to help you cut ten 7-inch (18 cm) lengths of wire. Cut a 3-inch (8 cm) strip of red tape. Lay the wire in the middle of the sticky side, a third of the way from the top. Then fold the top third down as shown.

2

▲ Trim the duct tape corners so they are rounded and petal-shaped.

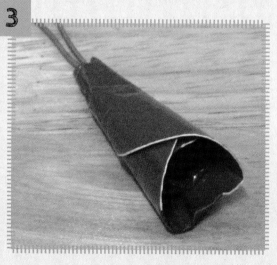

3

▲ Roll the petal tightly around into a bud shape.

4

▲ Make more petals and wrap them around your bud.

5

▲ Gently shape the petals by bending the wire outward.

6

▲ Color any white cut edges with red marker.

7

Wrap a strip of green tape around the stem.

MORE IDEAS

To make **sepals**, cut a small rectangle of green duct tape and fold the top over. Cut the green folded top into a triangle shape. Wrap the tape around the stem and gently fold the triangles outward.

Glossary

bookworm A person devoted to reading or study.

contrasting Showing noticeable differences.

cutting mat A flexible mat used for crafts and for cutting. The surface recloses afterward.

diagonally Running in a slanting direction.

embossed A design that has been carved, molded, or stamped on a surface or object.

excess More than necessary.

porcelain A hard white ceramic ware used especially for dishes and chemical utensils.

reversible Having two finished usable sides.

seal To join two things together so as to prevent them from coming apart.

sepals Specialized leaves that form part of a flower.

spray lubricant Grease or oil in a spray can.

taut Not slack.

washi tape A type of decorative colored adhesive tape.

water-resistant Able to resist the penetration of water to some degree but not entirely.

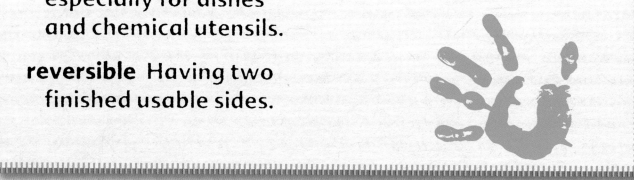

Further Information

Books

Bell-Rehwoldt, Sheri. *The Kids' Guide to Duct Tape Projects.* Mankato, MN: Capstone Press, 2012.

Bernhardt, Carolyn. *Duct Tape Fashion.* Minneapolis, MN: Lerner Publications, 2017.

Davis, Forest Walker. *Duct Tape: 101 Adventurous Ideas for Art, Jewelry, Flowers, Wallets and More.* Beverly, MA: Quarry Books, 2015.

Websites

Due to the changing nature of Internet links, PowerKids Press has developed an online list of websites related to the subject of this book. This site is updated regularly. Please use this link to access the list:
www.powerkidslinks.com/hbm/ducttape

Index